1 2 3 4 5 6 7 8   06 05 04 03 02

The Creepiest, Scariest, Weirdest Creatures Ever!

by
Mary Kay Carson

kidsbooks
Incorporated

Introduction

If getting creeped, scared, or weirded out is your idea of a good time, get ready for some fun! This book features some of nature's oddest animals in all their eye-popping glory. Every turn of the page will introduce you to another face that only a mother could love.

Once you get past the initial "Yuck!" reaction to the photos, you'll find even more fun in store: learning what that animal is, where it lives, and why it looks the way it does.

As creepy, scary, or weird as these animals may seem to us humans, it is important to remember that even the yuckiest of these creatures' features serves a useful purpose. Most help the animals survive in their natural environments—often, to catch food or to escape from being eaten themselves.

It also is important to remember that looking creepy, scary, or weird is not necessarily the same as being truly dangerous. Some are dangerous, of course: You would be wise to steer clear of a scorpion fish—its spines are always painful and sometimes poisonous. However, why worry about a praying mantis? It looks creepy and is deadly to the insects it hunts and eats, but it is no match for a human—even if it *wanted* to tangle with you!

Ready to meet the creepiest, scariest, weirdest creatures ever? All you have to do is turn the page.

Fangtooth

You don't have to worry about running into one of these fierce-looking fish. Fangtooths make their home in the very deep, dark part of the ocean. They can survive in frigid black waters as deep as three miles below the surface.

It is hard to find a meal in this Dark Zone, where there is no light, no plants, and few animals. Fangtooths eat shrimps, small fish, or anything else that happens by.

Fangtooths are also called ogre fish because they are so scary-looking. Many deep-sea fish look like monsters, with those huge mouths and long teeth, but this fangtooth is only six inches long!

A fangtooth's mouth and teeth ensure that it doesn't miss out on a meal. The big mouth enables this fish to gulp down whatever it finds, no matter what size the prey is. The long teeth curve inward, so nothing gets away. Young fangtooths have to wait a while to be such fierce hunters—only the adults have real fangs.

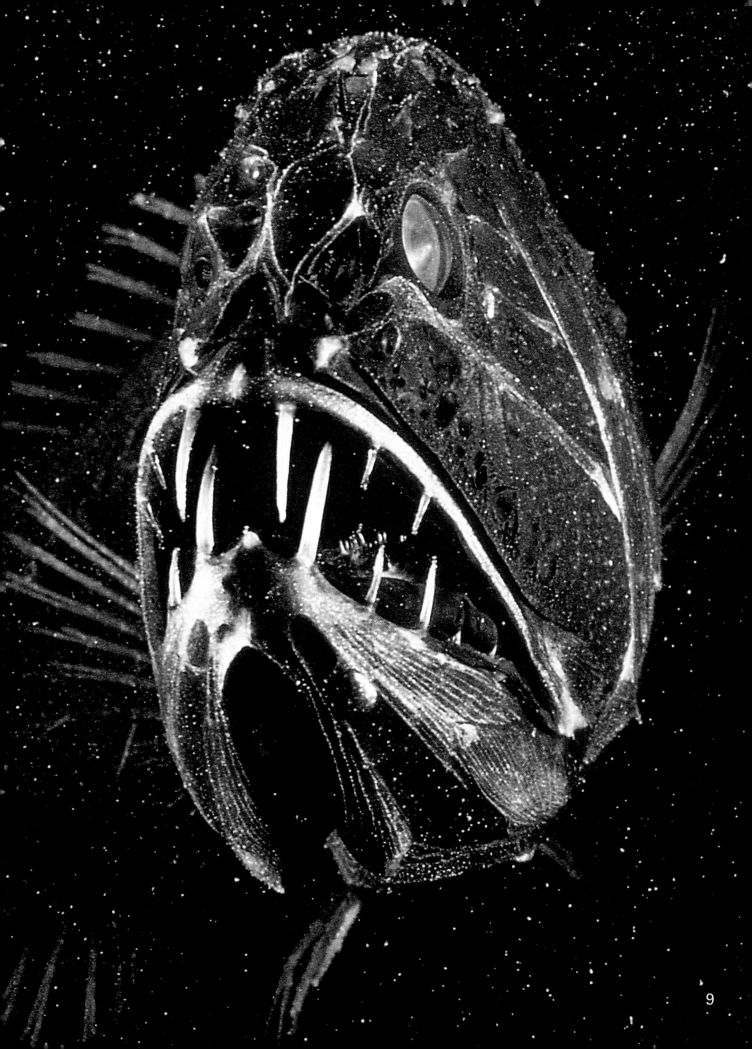

Spiders

All spiders are meat-eating predators, and built for the kill—like the spider above. That row of coldly staring eyes helps it spot prey, and all those tiny body hairs help it feel its way around in the dark.

Spiders may "bug" you, but they are not insects. (Spiders have eight legs, while insects have only six.) Spiders belong to their own eight-legged animal group called **arachnids** *(uh-RAK-nidz).*

How deadly is this skull-faced jumping spider? Very—to its prey. Spiders kill their victims with **venom** (poison) shot into the body with sharp fangs. Although all spiders are poisonous, very few have fangs that can break a person's skin, or poison strong enough to hurt humans.

Cuttlefish

Does this weird-faced creature have a really big nose? Not really—look again. What first appears to be a nose or beak is really the animal's arms!

This is a cuttlefish. Despite the name, it is not a fish. Cuttlefish are soft-bodied animals called **mollusks** *(MAHL-usks)*— the same family as squid and octopuses.

A cuttlefish has only one fin, which circles its body like a frilly skirt. It also has 10 arms that hang below its large eyes, surrounding its mouth. One pair of arms, called **tentacles** *(TEN-tuh-kulz),* is extra long. The cuttlefish uses the tentacles to grab small fish and crabs, which it eats. It uses its fin and the other arms to creep along the seafloor and sneak up on prey.

Cuttlefish are food for many other ocean creatures. (Humans find them tasty, too!) To hide, cuttlefish bury themselves in the sand. They also use **camouflage**— they can change the color of their skin to match their surroundings! If attacked, a cuttlefish squirts an inky fluid that darkens the water, hiding it long enough to escape.

Katydids

The alien-looking insect at right is only about two inches long. It is a katydid *(KAY-tee-did)*. Those two yellow stalks rising from its head, just above those bugged-out eyes, are the katydid's antennae *(an-TEN-ee),* or feelers. All insects have antennae. They use them to sense movement, smells, and heat.

This cone-head katydid has an extra feature: a sharp horn on its head. Any animal that tries to swallow it will really "get the point" not to try that again!

Katydids are insect cousins of grasshoppers and crickets. They eat leaves, grass, and young, tender twigs. Many katydids have a body shape and color that make them look like leaves. This helps protect them from hungry birds, bats, and lizards. This flat-face katydid has an extra-large face to help it scare away predators.

The katydid gets its name from the "kay-tee-did, kay-tee-did" love song that the males sing. A male sings by rubbing its front wings together. Little ridges on the wings make the sound. It is like rubbing two combs together.

15

Wolf Eel

Wolf eels—
also known as wolf-
fish—might look scary,
but they are harmless. Divers
even pet them!

The largest of this **species** (kind of animal) can get quite large—about
7.5 feet long. Wolf eels have powerful teeth, which they use to crunch up
their favorite foods: starfish, crabs, and sea urchins.

Tasmanian Blenny

Coral reefs are full of hungry predators. Besides keeping to its burrow for protection, the little five-inch-long Tasmanian blenny tries to look tough. Those "horns" growing above each eye help this scaleless fish look more fierce.

Blennies are small fish that live in oceans around the world. Most like shallower water, around kelp beds or coral reefs. Blennies that live around coral reefs, like this Tasmanian blenny, hang out in burrows for safety.

Tasmanian blennies live in the Indian Ocean around Tasmania and southeastern Australia. (Tasmania is a large island off the southeast coast of Australia.)

Weevils

This isn't a villain from a sci-fi movie. It's a weevil *(WEE-vul)*, a type of beetle with a long snout. In fact, the one on this page is called a snout beetle! Weevils are the largest family of beetles. There are more than 40,000 different kinds of weevils. Many weevils are pests that eat crops and damage flowers and trees.

This red-stripe weevil lives in Malaysia. You don't have to go that far to meet a weevil, however. They live all over the world, including many kitchens. Ever notice tiny bugs in a package of flour, crackers, or rice? They probably were little weevils!

Weevils use their snouts to eat their way into plant buds and seeds. A female weevil also uses her snout—often as long as her body—to drill holes in plants or seeds, then lays her eggs in the holes. When the young weevils hatch, they are in a room full of food!

19

Goosefish

There is nothing weird about this picture—as long as you think it's a mossy rock. Look again, though, and you'll see eyes, and a mouth with sharp teeth. That "rock" is a fish—a goosefish.

The goosefish is a hunter with an amazing camouflage job. Those things that look like vines and leaves are parts of its body! Unsuspecting prey that swim too close to this "garden" are in for a nasty shock.

Goosefish live in warm and temperate oceans around the world. An adult can weigh more than 100 pounds and reach six feet long.

Goosefish hide on the seafloor and lie in wait for prey. Small fish come looking for a bit of what they think is salad, only to be eaten as the main course! Goosefish eat mostly fish, but sometimes catch seabirds at the surface.

Speaking of meals, you may have eaten one of the two dozen or so kinds of goose-fish. At fish counters and on menus, it is called monkfish or "poor man's lobster."

Bats

Many people think that bats are spooky. That may be because bats are **nocturnal**—they are awake at night and do all their hunting in the dark. They spend daylight hours in dark caves or old attics. Despite their scary looks, bats help humans by eating lots of pest bugs, including mosquitoes.

Bats are the only mammals that can fly. A web of thin skin connects their arms, fingers, and legs, forming wings.

The toothy fellow below is a vampire bat—a type of bat that doesn't eat insects. It drinks blood instead! A vampire bat uses its large front teeth to bite into an animal, then laps up the blood with its tongue. Vampire bats have bitten humans, but they mostly feed on sleeping cows, pigs, and horses.

Bats—like the lobed forehead bat at left—may seem scary, but their weird features are very useful. A bat's giant ears and odd-shaped nose help it hunt and fly in the dark. Bats track down their prey using echolocation *(EK-oh-loh-KAY-shun):* The bat makes noises, then listens for the echoes to bounce back to its ears. The timing and sound of the echoes tell the bat what is where—including insects or other likely prey.

23

Lampreys

What is this messy mass of slime-covered creepy crawlers? Not worms. They are lampreys, primitive fish from 6 to 40 inches long, that lack scales, bony skeletons, or jaws. Lampreys start out as slimy, blind, and toothless **larvae** *(LAR-vee)*. (*Larvae* are the young forms of some animals.) Lamprey larvae live in muddy or sandy stream bottoms for several years, then grow into adults with eyes and teeth. The adults swim out to open waters, including freshwater lakes and northern oceans.

Lampreys are **parasites**—animals that live off of others. An adult lamprey's mouth is perfect for its job, built like a round suction cup with rows of horny teeth. The lamprey uses that mouth to latch on to a host fish. Then it uses its tooth-covered tongue to scrape open the fish's skin and suck out its blood and other body fluids.

25

Beetles

A beetle's mouth is built for the food it eats. These jaws of death belong to a tiger beetle.

Those large eyes keep watch for prey. When the tiger beetle spots small insects or spiders, it quickly flies or runs after them and—snap!—nabs the prey with its fierce, jagged-toothed mouth parts.

More than a quarter of a million different species of beetles live all over the planet—everywhere from hot rain forests and deserts to the cold Arctic. Some beetles are almost too small to see, while others are the size of your hand. Ladybugs and fireflies are beetles you may know.

26

The jaws of the long-horned beetle below are more of a tool than a weapon. Long-horned beetles are also known as wood-boring beetles for a good reason: They gnaw their way inside trees, where they lay their eggs. When the larvae hatch, they chomp away, eating as they tunnel their way back outside. Sometimes you can hear the young insects crawling inside wooden walls or furniture!

Scorpion Fish

Look closely! The weird-looking objects on these two pages are not underwater plants or rocks. They are scorpion fish, which live mostly in the Pacific Ocean. Can you spot the mouth and eye among the coral-reef camouflage on the scorpion fish above?

for scorpion fish, being mistaken for the ocean bottom or part of a coral reef is a useful trick. The scorpion fish's natural camouflage lets it disappear into the background, where it holds still and waits. When other fish, not realizing the danger, swim close enough, wham! The scorpion fish opens its mouth, snaps up that fish, and gulps it down.

Watch your step! You don't want to step on a scorpion fish. Many have long spines, and some scorpion-fish spines are poisonous. When a diver or swimmer steps on a spine, it shoots poison into the foot just like a needle. This scorpionlike sting is where the fish gets its name. A scorpion fish's poison is strong enough to cause breathing problems and can kill a human.

Robber Flies

What a face! It would be even scarier if you were a bee or a wasp—the robber fly's natural prey. A robber fly swoops down and grabs prey with its bristly legs. The fly kills the bee or wasp with a shot of poisonous spit from its pointy, stabbing mouth, then carries it to a favorite perch. There, the robber fly sucks out the bee's body juices. After the bee has been sucked dry, the fly tosses the dried-up body away.

There are about 5,000 different species of robber flies in the world. Robber flies hunt and eat all kinds of insects, including harmful pests. They will even eat other robber flies. That is why a male robber fly prefers to meet his mate when she is already eating—something else!

When a male robber fly wants to meet a female, he hovers above her, weaving back and forth. This odd-looking courtship display gets her attention.

31

Whitemargin Stargazer

One look at these pointy teeth, and you can guess that you're looking at a hunter—but what kind? This spooky, gravel-covered face belongs to a whitemargin stargazer—a type of fish. The name comes from the way this creature's eyes point straight up, as if it is gazing toward the sky.

Whitemargin stargazers live in the warm waters of the Pacific and Indian oceans. There, they spend most of their time buried in the sand or mud of the seafloor, waiting for a meal to swim by. When prey gets close enough, the stargazer leaps out, catching and swallowing it in one gulp.

Marine Iguana

This dinosaur look-alike is a marine iguana *(ih-GWAHN-uh)*, one of many weird creatures living on the Galápagos Islands of South America. Marine iguanas dive to the seafloor to eat seaweed there. While swimming and eating, a marine iguana swallows a lot of salt water. Special glands near its nose collect the extra salt, then the iguana sneezes it out through its nose. The sneezed-out salty spray shoots up in the air. It often falls back down on the iguana's head, making a white salt "wig" like this one. (These reptiles sneeze their salty snot at enemies and tourists, too!)

Thorny Devil

This fierce-looking reptile is a thorny devil, a small lizard that lives in the sandy Australian desert. Its main meal is ants. As dangerous as it may look, the thorny devil is a harmless creature, only about eight inches long. What looks like fearsome weaponry is just spiky armor that keeps this slow-moving creature safe from predators.

Hatchetfish

This small, googly-eyed creature is a hatchetfish. It lives in the Twilight Zone of the deep sea. Some daylight reaches its half-mile-deep ocean home, but not much. The name *hatchetfish* comes from this animal's thin, blade-like body shape.

Those big eyes help the hatchetfish see in the dim light. They work like a zoom lens on a camera, able to focus both close up and far away.

A hatchetfish has rows of pale blue glowing lights along its belly. When a predator swimming below looks up, all it sees is a faint light filtering down from the surface. This helps keep the three-inch hatchet-fish safely hidden.

Dragonfish

Some dragonfish glow in the dark! Glowing helps them see food and find mates.

Unlike most fish, dragonfish lack scales. Their bodies are covered with a jellylike layer full of light organs.

Most dragonfish have a long, glowing barbel (similar to a whisker) hanging from their chins. They use their barbels like fishing poles, luring little fish close to their long, pointy teeth. Dinner!

Dragonfish live in a very deep ocean area called the Dark Zone. It is so deep, sunlight never reaches it and the temperature is barely above freezing. Plants can't grow and few animals can survive there. Those that do, like the dragonfish, are very creepy-looking! Dragonfish are not giant monsters, though. Most are only four to six inches long.

Mantids

Mantids are fierce predatory insects with long legs and tiny heads. This one has nabbed a garden spider. Mantids use the sharp hooks at the ends of their front legs to hold prey tight while they eat.

The mantid—also known as a praying mantis—is the only type of insect able to turn its head from side to side. That comes in handy when scanning for prey! Some people buy mantid eggs and let them hatch in their gardens, because mantids are natural pest killers.

A mantid's shape and color help it hide while it waits for prey. Some—like the dead-leaf mantid below—look like leaves. Others look more like green twigs or brown knotty sticks. Some mantids live in cool parts of Europe and North America, but most live in the tropics and other warm places.

39

Frogfish

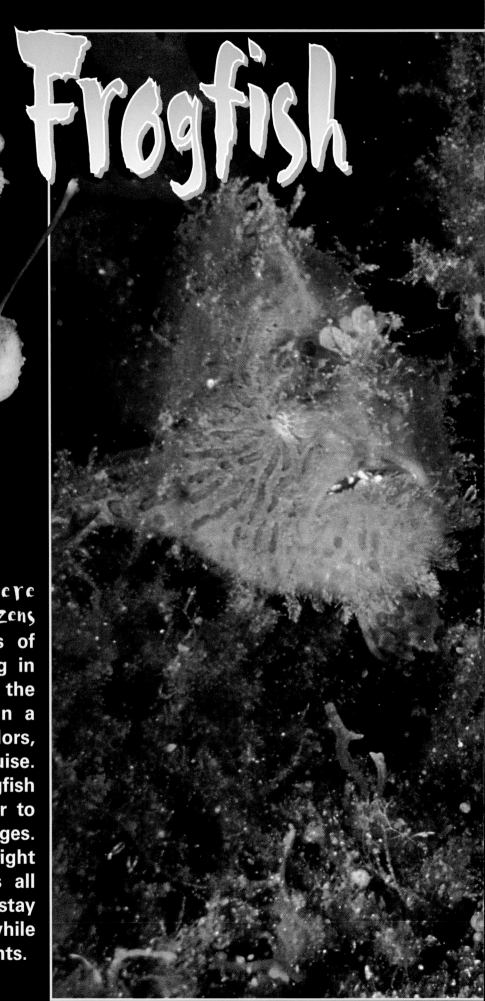

There are dozens of species of frogfish, living in warm oceans all around the globe. Frogfish come in a variety of sizes and colors, and are masters of disguise. The lumpy longlure frogfish above changes its color to look like the local sponges. The striated frogfish at right have plantlike growths all over, which help them stay perfectly camouflaged while fishing in clumps of plants.

Each frogfish has a "fishing pole" growing out of its head with a fleshy lure on the end. Some lures look like worms; others, like shrimp. Some even look like tiny fish, complete with eyelike spots! Sometimes prey bite off a lure before the frogfish catches the prey. The lure will grow back, but the frogfish may go hungry in the meantime.

Striated frogfish can swallow water to puff themselves up, which makes them look bigger to predators.

Slugs

What is this slithery, slimy-looking thing? It is a slug—a snail without a shell. Slugs belong to the soft-bodied mollusk family.

Slugs live around the world, usually in damp, cool, shady places. They spend sunny days hiding under leaves or rotting logs, eating fungi and rotting leaves. (This slug is munching on a mushroom.) Some slug species eat meat— other snails, as well as earthworms.

Slug slime, which is like mucus, protects the animal from hungry enemies. When a bird or other predator tries to eat a slug, the slug oozes extra slime out through its skin. Most animals hate the way a gooey slug feels in their mouths, so they spit it out.

43

Anglerfish

Food is hard to come by in the dark, deep ocean, and swimming around looking for prey uses up a lot of energy. That is why these deep-sea fish wait for food to come to them.

An anglerfish catches food by using a fishing pole that grows out of its head. The glowing tip of this special fishing-rod fin acts as a lure. (The tip glows because it is filled with millions of light-making bacteria.) The anglerfish wiggles this lure to attract its prey. When a fish, shrimp, or other deep-sea creature swims too close to the light, the anglerfish swallows its meal whole. It can gulp down prey nearly as large as itself, thanks to its wide mouth and expanding stomach.

Caterpillars

A caterpillar may look like a worm, but it is the larva of a moth or butterfly. A caterpillar eventually goes through a change called **metamorphosis** *(MET-uh-MORE-fuh-sus)*. It spins a cocoon around its body. Then, while hidden away inside, it changes into a moth or butterfly.

A caterpillar's job is to eat, eat, and eat some more. It can't spin a cocoon until it is fat enough! Most caterpillars gorge themselves on tree leaves.

While eating, a caterpillar wants to escape from being eaten itself! Many caterpillars have ways of hiding from hungry birds and other predators. Hairy gypsy moth caterpillars, like the one below, lie low during the day. At night, they move up into trees to eat leaves. Other caterpillars are camouflaged by their color or shape.

The hickory horned devil (above) is the caterpillar of the regal moth (see p. 54). Check out this caterpillar's pointy spines. They make a predator think twice before trying to swallow it!

Moray Eels

Eels look like underwater snakes. They aren't reptiles, though; they are fish. Most eels don't have scales. Their skin is covered in a protective layer of slippery mucus instead.

There are many different kinds of eels, and many varieties of each kind. The fish you see on these two pages are moray eels—just two of at least 80 different moray species.

Moray eels are hunters. They hide in the cracks and holes of coral reefs. When a fish or squid swims by, a moray will pop out and bite it. Don't try petting a moray eel. It will give any bothersome visitor a nasty bite. Don't try biting back, either! Some morays are safe to eat, but the flesh of others can make humans sick—or even kill them.

The two dragon moray eels at left aren't laughing or showing off their dental work. They have such long teeth that they can't close their mouths!

Condor

The California condor is one of the largest flying birds in the world. It has a wingspan of 8 to 9.5 feet!

Condors are large vultures. Like all vultures, they eat **carrion** (dead animals). That bald condor head is perfect for poking into dead bodies. A feathered head would just get covered in blood and rotting guts. Most vultures also keep clean by pooping on their own feet and legs. Their droppings are very acidic, which helps to kill germs.

This bird may look creepy, but you would be lucky to see one. The California condor almost became extinct. Today, only about 150 survive. Most of those live in captivity, but scientists are trying to release the birds into the wild.

Uakari

The
bald uakari is
a mammal that
lives in the swampy
forests along the
Amazon River in South
America. It spends its
days high in the trees
eating fruit, nuts, and
leaves. Amazonian
Indians capture young
uakaris for pets, but
kill and eat the
adults.

The Amazon rain
forest is home to mon-
keys of many shapes,
colors, and sizes. The bald
uakari *(wah-KAH-ree)* is
one of the more odd-looking
monkeys that live there. Not only is it bald and
scarlet-skinned, but it has a short tail. All other
monkeys of the Americas have long tails.

Pacific Giant Octopus

This creature, the Pacific giant octopus, is the largest octopus in the world. This mollusk can weigh 100 pounds and measure 20 feet from arm tip to arm tip! (The world's smallest octopus is a lot smaller—only an inch across.)

The Pacific giant octopus's main diet is crabs and lobsters, but it has been known to eat bigger fish—even sharks!

An octopus can swim fast when it needs to. It jet-propels itself backward by shooting water out of its body. An octopus can also squirt an inky liquid at an enemy. The ink darkens the water, hiding the octopus and giving it time to swim to safety.

An octopus is all head, tentacles, and eyes. The underside of each of its eight tentacles is covered in suction cups. An octopus uses its sucker-covered tentacles to catch prey along the bottom of the sea. If an octopus loses an arm, it just grows a new one.

Moths smell their way to food. They sip juice from fruits or nectar from flowers using a long strawlike mouth. The mouth coils up under the moth's head when it is finished drinking. Look closely at this regal moth's face, and you will see its partly coiled mouth.

Moths

These big-eyed bugs are moths—insects related to butterflies, but more different than you may realize. For one thing, moths are nocturnal, while butterflies are daytime flyers. Moths are usually fatter and fuzzier. As for antennae, a butterfly's look like slim stalks with knobs on the end, while a moth's are wider near the head and narrower at the ends. Some—like those of the luna moth *(below)*—look like feathers or fern fronds. All those tiny antenna hairs pick up smells. They are so sensitive, a male moth can smell a female that is five miles away!

Batfish

Is this a crab, a bug, or a frog? None of the above! It's a batfish. The batfish is a small, strange-looking fish with a flat head. It is covered with hard lumps and spiny scales. Batfish walk on the ocean bottom using armlike fins as legs. They can swim, but not very gracefully!

The batfish has a lure-tipped fishing pole growing out of its head. Unlike other kinds of lure-equipped fish, however, the batfish's "fishing pole" is retractable—when not in use, the batfish draws it up inside a tube.

Most kinds of batfish live in the deep sea, but this red-lipped batfish lives in shallow waters around reefs off South America's Galápagos Islands.

Cryptic Frogfish

There are many types of frogfish (see pp. 40-41). The one below is a cryptic frogfish. *Cryptic* means "hidden." All frogfish are good at hiding themselves, but the cryptic frogfish also hides its egg clusters—in a pocket formed by bending its tail fin around to its shoulder fin.

Microscopic Creatures

The animal above is a deer tick, a creature related to spiders. All those legs help this parasite hang on to its host as it sucks its blood. Deer ticks mostly feed on deer and wild mice, but sometimes on humans. A deer tick's bite can transfer Lyme disease from infected animals to humans.

Some of the creepiest creatures around are too small to see with just your eyes. You would need a microscope to get a close look.

The microscopic creatures on these two pages are parasites—they live by feeding off of other animals.

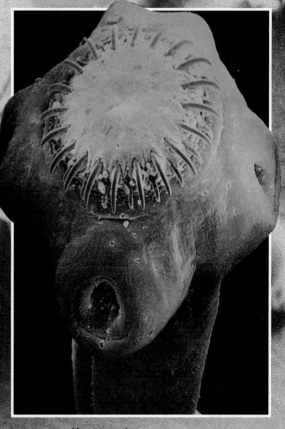

Not all parasites live outside the host animal's body. Some, like this tapeworm, live inside it! Tapeworms live inside the gut of an animal—including humans. That crown of hooks on its head is how it holds on to its host.

The smallest tapeworms are only about 0.04 inch long. A few, however, can grow much bigger than microscope size— about 50 feet long. (A tapeworm like that would need a pretty big host!)

Photo Credits

American Fisheries Society: p. 25
Bill Beatty: pp. 10-11, 26, 30, 38, 46-47, 54
DRK: Michael Fogden/DRK: p. 23
François Gohier: pp. 50, 51
Dwight R. Kuhn: p. 55
Minden Pictures: *Fred Bavendam*—pp. 16, 17, 32-33, 40-41, 52-53, 53 (inset), 56-57, 57 (inset); *Frans Lanting*— pp. 14, 34, 35; *Mark Moffett*—pp. 10, 27; *Flip Nicklin*—p. 49 (inset); *Dr. Bruce Robison*—pp. 8-9, 44-45
Robert & Linda Mitchell: pp. 15, 19, 31, 39, 42-43, 43 (inset)
Photo Researchers, Inc: *Rexford Lord*—front cover/p. 22
Jeff Rotman Photography: pp. 20-21, 28
A. B. Sheldon: pp. 24, 47
Visuals Unlimited: *Chris Crowley*—p. 40; *David B. Fleetham*—pp. 29, 48-49/back cover; *HBOI*—p. 37; *David M. Phillips*—pp. 58-59; *Kjell B. Sandved*—p. 18; *G. Shih-R. Kessel*—p. 59; *David Wrobel*—pp. 12-13
Norbert Wu: p. 36

Index